Betsy—
Hope this brings
back wonderful memories for
you — Happy Birthday :)
Kathy

ENGLAND

GALLERY BOOKS
An Imprint of W. H. Smith Publishers Inc.
112 Madison Avenue
New York City 10016

This edition first published in U.S.
in 1991 by Gallery Books,
an imprint of W.H. Smith Publishers, Inc.
112 Madison Avenue, New York, New York 10016

ISBN 0-8317-0262-1

Printed and bound in Spain

For rights information about the photographs in
this book please contact:

The Image Bank
111 Fifth Avenue, New York, NY 10003

Producer: Solomon M. Skolnick
Writer: Nancy Millichap Davies
Design Concept: Lesley Ehlers
Designer: Ann-Louise Lipman
Editor: Joan E. Ratajack
Production: Valerie Zars
Photo Researcher: Edward Douglas
Assistant Photo Researcher: Robert V. Hale
Editorial Assistant: Carol Raguso

Title page: This pub sign reflects the
prosperity of medieval England, which
was based on the wool trade. *Opposite:*
St. Paul's, the City of London's cathedral,
rises from its reflection in the Thames to
dominate the glittering skyline in this
sunset view.

To visitors, the most striking thing about England is the visible persistence of the past. At every turn, you see evidence of the country's long and colorful history. You can walk along a London street that follows the path and bears the name of a stream rerouted underground centuries ago. Mailing a postcard, you may see "Victoria" or "George V" embossed on the side of a red "posting box" and discover it's the name of the monarch in whose reign the posting box was cast and installed. Or if you pop into a country pub for a "pint," you'll often find low ceilings and a large, open fireplace that are not reproductions but original features of the pub's construction three, four, or five centuries ago.

Rural England has long been agricultural wherever the land will support crops. It is a country where almost every landscape gives some sign of shaping by human hands. Your first impression of England from the air is likely to be of a pattern of tidy green squares, bordered in deeper green. Close up, the "quilt" reveals itself to be fields bordered by hedgerows. Even in the days when the legendary Robin Hood and his band roamed Sherwood Forest, the forest was not a dense wood, but an environment of mixed forest and open pastureland reserved for royal hunts. Today, 330 square miles of Sherwood remain, carefully guarded against overdevelopment, a green retreat for the residents of nearby Nottingham.

Above: The Whispering Gallery, so named because a whisper on one side is clearly audible 100 feet away on the opposite side, circles beneath the frescoed dome. *Left:* High Altar has been the scene of many public ceremonies including the wedding of Prince Charles and Lady Diana Spencer.

Above, left to right: Bronze Justice, without a blindfold, holds her scales and sword 215 feet above ground atop Old Bailey, the Central Criminal Court. The Old Bailey houses 23 different courts, including Court Number One, where some of Britain's most infamous criminals of the twentieth century have been tried. *Below:* The Bank of England, popularly known as the Old Lady of Threadneedle Street, vies with the Royal Mercantile Exchange for attention.

This postmodern building is the home of Lloyd's insurance market. *Below:* Its interior showcases structural elements such as the steel frame and ductwork. *Opposite:* A consortium of independent insurance investors started in a coffeehouse in the late seventeenth century, Lloyd's is famous for, but by no means limited to, marine insurance.

Who were the first humans to shape the English landscape? We know little of them, but a group or groups of prehistoric people left unmistakable traces including the great stone circles of Avebury and Stonehenge, as well as other, less heavily visited standing stones throughout the western part of the country. Today no one is certain of the reasons behind the building of these circles, which seem to have been neither dwelling areas nor graveyards. Some of the archaeologists and mystics who study them believe that rites related to fertility and the burial of the dead took place within the rings. Stonehenge, the best known of these megalithic creations, has an unusual feature: The paired stones are joined with stone "lintels." In other circles, each great stone stands independently. Regardless of whether the stones are joined or not, visitors wonder at the powerful sense of mystery that they radiate.

England is an island country, sharing Great Britain with Wales to the west and Scotland to the north. Each of these culturally distinct lands is administratively a part of the nation known by the lengthy title of "The United Kingdom of Great Britain and Northern Ireland." The broad, gray belt of encircling sea has served so well as a defensive moat that England has not been successfully invaded for nearly a thousand years.

Earlier in the country's history, however, various invaders from the European mainland crossed the English Channel and the North Sea. First came the Celts, a tall and fair

Preceding page: Beefeaters provide ceremonial security at the Tower of London. The thistle, rose, and shamrock on their uniforms represent the united kingdoms of Scotland, England, and Northern Ireland. *This page, above:* The eleventh-century White Tower is the central keep of the old fortress. *Right:* If the Tower's ravens ever leave, legend proclaims, England will fall.

◄ Jewel House

◄ White Tower

Beauchamp T

These pages: Tower Bridge, completed in 1894, spans the Thames to connect North and South London. A steel frame supports its weighty stone facing. A symbolic sculpture in front of the bridge recalls London's maritime heritage.

Above: Knights' effigies lie in Temple Church, which was built by the Knights Templar, a crusading order of medieval times. *Below, left:* The Coliseum in St. Martin's Lane, London's largest theater, is home to the English National Opera. *Right:* A marble statue of William Shakespeare stands in Leicester Square. *Opposite:* In the center of Trafalgar Square, a traditional site for political rallies and demonstrations, Nelson's Column rises 145 feet to commemorate the naval hero of the Napoleonic Wars.

THERE IS
NO DARKNESS
BUT
IGNORANCE

people who had the use of horses and iron tools. Historians surmise that their metal weapons gave them easy mastery of the inhabitants they found in Britain. Archaeologists report that, once established, the Celts lived in villages of round wooden huts. Evidence of a village of dozens of such huts remains beneath the site of Glastonbury Abbey, itself now fallen into romantic, high-arched ruins. The Celtic culture, with its rich storytelling traditions and its Druid-led religion of nature worship and magic, was the dominant one in the years before the beginning of the Christian era. Celtic remains in England today include magnificent metal artifacts such as the Battersea Shield, which was found in London's river Thames and is now displayed in the British Museum, and the huge Uffington White Horse in Oxfordshire, a 365-foot-long outline of a horse cut through the turf of a hillside and into the underlying chalk.

Just before the beginning of the Christian era the Celtic villages and their larger, earthwork-protected hill forts fell before the next invaders, the Romans, who also left their marks on the landscape. Modern motorways, including the Great North Road that leads from London into the heart of the country, often follow the arrow-straight pathways over which Roman chariots once rolled. As colonizers, the Romans needed a strong military presence to maintain control of their province of Britannia. *Castra,* the Latin word for camp, survives today in the many place names ending with *-chester, -cester,* or *-caster*—all onetime Roman bases. But Celtic

This page, top to bottom: A lion and a unicorn grace the pediment of the church of St. Martin-in-the-Fields (1724), the Royal Parish Church overlooking Trafalgar Square. A 20-foot-long bronze lion, one of four flanking Nelson's column, seems to guard the National Gallery in this shot. Water jets spout from the bronze inhabitants of a granite fountain in the square.

resistance grew stronger as the Romans moved northward. After many fierce battles in the region of what today is the border between England and Scotland, the Romans built the 73-mile-long Hadrian's Wall to protect themselves from the fiercest of the Celtic people. Today, remains of the wall and its forts stretch along a band of lonely Northumberland countryside.

The Romans were accomplished builders, mostly working in stone, and Hadrian's Wall, the onetime northern boundary of the Roman Empire, is only one of many relics of that ancient time. In London, visitors can see the remnants of the original walls of the Roman settlement of Londinium. These walls later served as the base for the city's medieval walls. Roman soldiers were sometimes given English lands in which to settle after leaving the army. A Roman bathhouse and the ruins of a temple to Minerva can be visited in aptly named Bath, the eighteenth-century spa town more famous for its crescent-shaped streets lined by limestone Palladian townhouses. Visitors to Fishbourne, near Chichester, can see the mosaic pavements, the baths, and even the reconstructed gardens of a Roman palace that apparently covered ten acres.

In the early fifth century, the Roman garrisons retreated back to the continent to defend their falling empire, leaving behind a country now transformed by reading, writing, and Christianity. However, new invaders were quick to cross the North Sea. The Angles, Saxons, and Jutes came from the regions that are now Germany and Denmark.

This page, top to bottom: Admiralty Arch (1910), is the ceremonial entrance to The Mall, which connects Trafalgar Square with Buckingham Palace. Number 10 Downing Street is the official residence of the prime minister. The shape of the Cenotaph in Whitehall, a memorial to World War I dead, is slightly convex and concave, and represents infinity.

Sunset and floodlights sculpt the Palace of Westminster in this view from the South Bank of the Thames. *Below:* The Houses of Parliament (1860) front the Thames. *Opposite:* Within the clock tower of the Palace of Westminster hangs the 13-ton Great Bell of Westminster, "Big Ben."

Auguste Rodin's bronze, *The Burghers of Calais,* stands in Victoria Tower Gardens, west of Parliament on the Thames. *Below:* In the yard of the Palace of Westminster is a likeness of the crusader king, Richard the Lion-hearted. *Opposite:* Westminster Abbey is the site of coronation as well as monuments to royalty and great commoners alike.

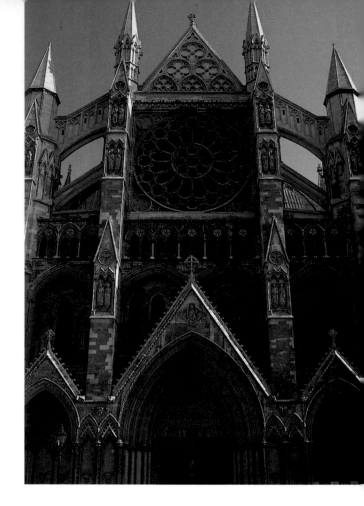

Above, left to right: Queen Elizabeth I and Mary Queen of Scots lie entombed in the abbey's Lady Chapel. Many of England's most famous architects have contributed to the Gothic architecture evidenced in the south transept of Westminster Abbey. *Below:* The Tate Gallery is the home of the national collection of modern paintings and British art of all periods.

Above: In St. James's Park, concertgoers lazily await the opening notes. *Right:* A flower bed in St. James's Park enlivens the Foreign Office in the background.

Preceding page: A member of a crack guards regiment, this sentry inside the gates at Buckingham Palace wears a full-dress uniform complete with bearskin hat. *This page, above:* Queen Victoria was the first monarch to live in Buckingham Palace, the 600-room London residence of the sovereign. *Below:* The Trooping of the Colour is an annual ceremony that marks the sovereign's birthday.

This page: Beaux-arts opulence is the hallmark of Harrods, one of the world's largest stores, located in fashionable Knightsbridge. *Opposite:* This statue at Hyde Park Corner honors the duke of Wellington, who defeated Napoleon at Waterloo.

Above, left to right: The Royal Albert Hall in Kensington is a gathering place for lovers of classical music. This frieze illustrates the triumph of arts and letters. The Albert Memorial in Kensington Gardens commemorates Queen Victoria's beloved husband, whom she outlived by 40 years. *Below:* Dinosaur skeletons haunt the Central Hall of the Natural History Museum in London's Richmond section. *Opposite:* Only members of the Royal Family and one elite cavalry troop may pass through Marble Arch (1827) at the northeast corner of Hyde Park.

England takes its name from the first of these groups: Over the years, "Angle-Land" contracted to "England." Wooden Anglo-Saxon buildings did not survive, although oak posts from this period form the walls of the church at Greensted-juxta-Ongar. The visitor who wants to get a sense of Anglo-Saxon England might well go to the British Museum in London to view the rich hoard of grave goods found in a ship burial at Sutton Hoo on the country's eastern coast and the Lindisfarne Gospels, a set of detailed illuminated manuscripts.

England was invaded successfully for the last time in 1066, when William the Conqueror, a nobleman from Normandy with a claim to the English throne, defeated Harold, the last Saxon king, at the Battle of Hastings. The Norman presence exerted a strong influence on English language and culture. For the visitor today, perhaps the most striking visual reminder of the Norman arrival is the Tower of London, which stands beside the Thames in what is now the city's East End. It served its builder, William the Conqueror, as both a military stronghold and a palace. Later the Tower became the most famous of the country's prisons. Among those to be held there were Sir Thomas More, Sir Walter Raleigh, and Henry VIII's unfortunate second queen, Anne Boleyn. Today it is a top destination for London visitors, both because of its grim history and because the Crown Jewels are kept there in an underground vault, guarded by warders called Beefeaters, whose style of uniform dates from Tudor times.

Above: The first public buses began running in London in 1829; this bus runs on approximately the same route as the first bus did. *Left:* Tourists and locals alike can choose from a variety of London street and Underground signs for sale as souvenirs.

No structures from the English Middle Ages are more glorious than the country's cathedrals. From the Romanesque rounded arches of Durham to the pure Gothic unity of Salisbury, they stand as tributes to an era of profound religious faith, a time when the identity of the individual was less important than the advancement of Christianity. The cathedrals are, by and large, the unsigned works of innumerable English artisans of great talent. Every visitor will have a particular favorite—Lichfield with its finely detailed carvings and its three spires, Lincoln with its dramatic hilltop setting, Wells with its peaceful cloisters. St. Paul's Cathedral in London, where Charles, Prince of Wales, married Lady Diana Spencer in 1981, is among the most visited. Rebuilt on the site of an earlier St. Paul's that was destroyed by the Great Fire of 1666, the current domed structure is the work of the famous architect Sir Christopher Wren, who is buried in its crypt.

Oxford and Cambridge, the two oldest universities in the English-speaking world, represent another highly visible legacy of the Middle Ages, one which continues to evolve to meet modern needs. The universities, each made up of a collection of individual colleges, developed as centers for the education of clergymen. Within high walls, each college contains a chapel, a library, and a "hall" or dining room, as well as student living quarters. Among the many remarkable structures in these university towns is King's College Chapel, in Cambridge. Begun by King Henry VI in the late fifteenth century, King's is England's last and greatest medieval building.

The Strand Theatre was built in 1905 in the West End, London's theater district. *Right:* Royal images at Madame Tussaud's Wax Museum on Baker Street include the Prince and Princess of Wales, Queen Elizabeth II, Prince Philip, and the duke and duchess of York.

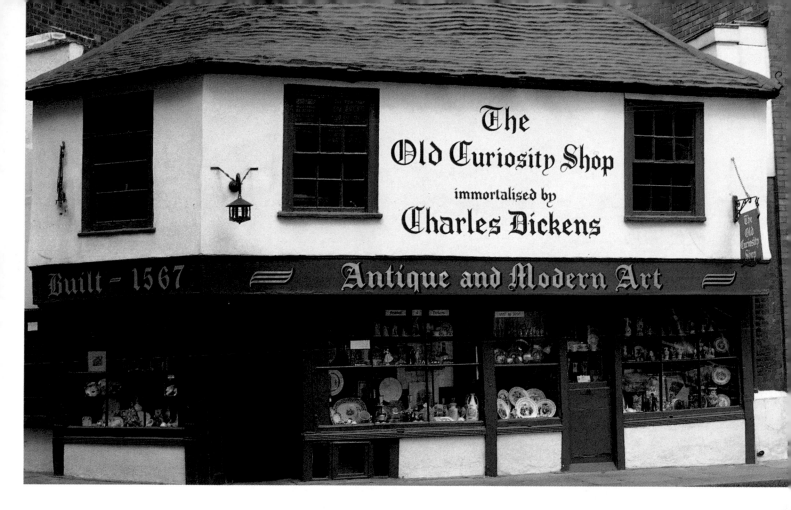

Preceding page: Neon signs jostle Regency period facades in Piccadilly Circus. *This page, above:* This Portsmouth Street shop, the oldest surviving shop in London, was built about 1567. Charles Dickens immortalized it as the home of his heroine, Little Nell. *Right:* A few fragments of the Roman walls that once encircled London still remain.

These pages: Heraldic beasts stand guard at Hampton Court. Cardinal Wolsey, once Henry VIII's most powerful subject, built this Thames-side palace 15 miles west of London in the early 1500's. Hampton Court's "new" sections were added by the distinguished architect Sir Christopher Wren in the late 1600's. *Overleaf:* Windsor Castle, the residence of English kings and queens since the Norman Conquest, lies west of London on the banks of the Thames. Twelve surrounding counties are visible from the 80-foot battlements of its Round Tower.

The future George IV built his seaside retreat, the Royal Pavilion, in a fanciful Oriental style in Brighton, on England's southern coast. *Below:* The Front, or Promenade, at Brighton recalls the elegance of an earlier era.

Right: Elizabeth I's portrait supplies the name for the Queen's Head Pub in Rye, a medieval seaport now several miles inland from the English Channel. *Below:* Hotels and shops line a street in a Kentish market town. *Following pages, left:* Canterbury Cathedral in the county of Kent, southeast of London, was the journey's end for the pilgrims of Chaucer's fourteenth-century *Canterbury Tales. Right:* Armorial bearings adorn fifteenth-century fan vaulting above a Canterbury Cathedral cloister.

Roses, crisply carved in stone, adorn its fan-vaulted interior walls.

The reign of Henry VIII's red-haired daughter Elizabeth, the "Virgin Queen," marked one of England's most brilliant and productive eras. The worst of the religious conflicts that had divided the country during the reign of her father had, for the time being, been resolved. English naval power triumphed against the might of the Spanish Armada, and outposts of English influence were established in Asia and North America. In the ensuing climate of national pride and prosperity, literary and artistic culture blossomed. The stern city fathers of London wanted nothing so frivolous as theaters within their walls, but across the Thames in Southwark, theaters flourished. Among the many popular playwrights of the day was a glover's son from the market town of Stratford-upon-Avon, William Shakespeare.

The theaters closed after England's Civil War in the mid-seventeenth century and stayed closed during the Commonwealth period that followed. The strict, Calvinist followers of Oliver Cromwell, who became Lord Protector of England after Charles I was executed, frowned on such "immorality." However, when the monarchy was restored in the 1660's, the theaters reopened.

Preceding pages: The Seven Sisters, a formation in the white chalk cliffs west of Dover, is the first sight of England for visitors from the European mainland. *This page, above:* Sir Christopher Wren designed Christ Church's Tom Tower, a seventeenth-century addition to the sixteenth-century Tom Quad, the oldest quadrangle in Oxford. The top of Carfax Tower at the crossroads of Queen and Cornmarket streets provides a panoramic view of Oxford. *Below:* Thomas, Earl of Pembroke, a benefactor of Oxford University, stands in bronze before the institution's Bodleian Library.

Above, left to right: St. John's College, Cambridge, was founded in 1511 by the mother of Henry VIII. The ornate pinnacles of King's College rise above Cambridge. *Below:* The Radcliffe Camera, Oxford, is the home of an undergraduate library.

Sunrise over the central altar at Stonehenge, Wiltshire, creates a dramatic effect. *Below:* Trilithons, crosspieces that join pairs of monoliths in the outer circle, make the mysterious site unique among Britain's many prehistoric rings of standing stones.

Today England is one of the world's great centers of theater. One hub of dramatic activity is the National Theater, on the south bank of the Thames which once was home to Shakespeare's Globe Theater. Musicals and dramas that open near the Thames's other shore, in London's West End, frequently go on to long Broadway runs. The Royal Shakespeare Company performs the plays of England's greatest playwright at several sites, including a theater at the 1982 Barbican Center in the East End and at the Royal Shakespeare Theater in Stratford-upon-Avon. Those who attend a performance there may also visit Shakespeare's birthplace, the cottage in nearby Shottery where he probably paid court to his wife, Anne Hathaway, and his grave in the parish church.

The London that for so long has been the heart of the English theater is also by far the most frequently visited of England's cities. Like most large cities with long histories, it is more a collection of distinctive and highly individual districts than a monolithic unit. First there is the City of London, the mile-square piece of land that was once enclosed by the medieval walls. The former center of all commerce, it is now the financial district. Westminster is farther to the west along the banks of the Thames, which bisects the city. It was historically the seat of government. Today the river there serves as a reflecting pool for the neo-Gothic buildings of the Mother of Parliaments. Nearby stands ancient Westminster Abbey, site of the coronation of every monarch since William the Conqueror. Geoffrey Chaucer, Samuel Johnson, Charles Dickens, and Thomas Hardy, among others, are buried in Poets' Corner in the abbey's south transept, where memorial stones honor many other poets and writers.

Salisbury Cathedral's 400-foot spire is the highest in England. *Right:* Once a royal stronghold, Corfe Castle, Dorset fell into ruins after its 1646 capture by Parliamentary forces during England's Civil War.

Dunster Castle and this outbuilding in Somerset are now owned by the National Trust, but previously belonged to one family for 600 years. *Below:* The State House at Lands End, Cornwall, stands atop the wild cliffs that distinguish the westernmost extremity of England.

Between the City and Westminster, and for miles in every direction, sprawls today's London, a bustling, international city. Sites that demand a visitor's attention include the British Museum in Bloomsbury, home of a rich treasure of cultural artifacts from England and around the world, the National Gallery with its Old Master paintings, the Tate Gallery, where a recently designed suite of exhibition halls shows off the national collection of the works of the great early-nineteenth-century English painter J. M. W. Turner, and the Victoria and Albert Museum with its renowned collection of decorative arts.

"When a man is tired of London, he is tired of life," Samuel Johnson remarked. Although visitors may not quickly tire of London, there are features of England, such as the celebrated castles, which they must go farther afield to see. The country's castles have more in common with army bases than mansions. Built in large part during the Middle Ages, they enabled the feudal lord and lady and their dependents to gather for safety during an invasion. Famous examples range from the ruins of Corfe in Dorset, a once-royal castle that fell to the Parliamentary party during the Civil War, to small, well-preserved Bodiam Castle in southern England, built in 1385 to stave off a French invasion that never happened.

The Queen of England has several residences, notably Buckingham Palace in London with its famous Changing of the Guard ceremony, but royal associations go

This page, top to bottom: Hot mineral springs led Britain's Roman colonizers to build a resort at Bath in the first century of the Christian era; the restored Roman baths survive today. Bath Abbey's stained-glass windows are the reason the abbey became known as "the lantern of the west." From the outside, Bath's Pulteney Bridge is just a span over the River Avon, but inside it's a fashionable shopping street.

back furthest at Windsor Castle, in the Royal Borough of Windsor west of London. Although it has been the monarch's primary residence since Norman times, Windsor's "great house" splendors far outshine its original function as a secure fortress in the minds of the thousands of people from abroad and from Queen Elizabeth II's own domains who visit the royal castle. Tours focus on the splendid state apartments, such as the Throne Room and the great Reception Room, and include the Albert Memorial Chapel, within which bronze-winged angels support the marble effigy of Prince Albert, Victoria's beloved consort. When members of the royal family—or "royals," as the English often call them—are in residence, a flag flies above the castle.

Preceding page: Broadway Tower rises from the summit of a Cotswold ridge. *This page, above:* Blenheim was built for an eighteenth-century general, the duke of Marlborough, to commemorate his defeat of Louis XIV's forces on the Danube at the town of the same name. *Below:* Marlborough's descendant, Sir Winston Churchill, was born here in 1874.

Royals have their castle at Windsor and their Buckingham Palace in the heart of London; other titled aristocrats have grand country houses. Or had them, in any case. The financial burden of maintaining the lavish rural seats established by their ancestors has, in many instances, led today's aristocrats to open their houses to tourists. For instance, Longleat, the marquess of Bath's Renaissance house in Wiltshire, is not only open to view but also has seals in its lake and a lion reserve within its grounds, to attract paying guests. In some cases, the stately homes have been given outright to the nation or to the National Trust, a private organization that acquires, opens to the public, and maintains historic and natural sites throughout the country.

The National Trust preserves such treasures as Belton House in Lincolnshire, considered the highest achievement of seventeenth-century domestic architecture, and Petworth House in its beautiful 700-acre deer park, among dozens of other properties. The Trust also purchases and protects wildlands—71 miles of coastal land in Devon, for instance, and a remarkable 140,000 acres in the picturesque Lake District in Cumbria that includes Scafell Pike, England's highest mountain. The Lake District was a favorite haunt of the romantic poets of the early nineteenth century, who would surely be pleased at the preservation of the misty grandeur that inspired them.

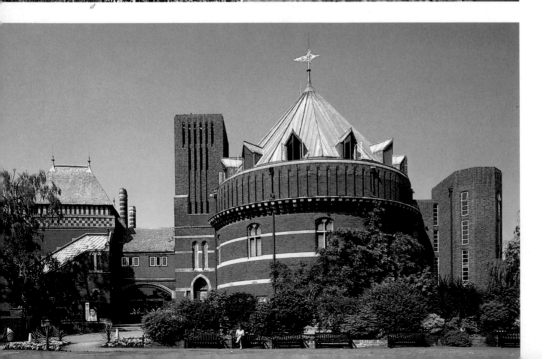

This page, top to bottom: The Warwickshire market town of Stratford-upon-Avon is known throughout the world as Shakespeare's birthplace. Anne Hathaway's cottage at nearby Shottery was the girlhood home of Shakespeare's wife. The Swan Theatre, one of the principal performance stages of the Royal Shakespeare Company, is built in the style of an Elizabethan playhouse. *Opposite:* Lincoln Cathedral, which was created primarily in the Gothic style, houses one of the four remaining originals of the Magna Carta.

Even in Cumbria, one of England's northernmost counties, the climate is noted for its moderation. Throughout the country, the gentle rains, fine mists, mild winters, and cool summers foster the cultivation of flowers and other ornamental plants. Formal gardens developed at every period since the Middle Ages flourish and can still be visited today. In many of them, a few roses are still blooming at Christmastime. Among the best gardens created in this century are those at Sissinghurst Castle in Sussex, where Vita Sackville-West used flowers to create elegant, painterly effects between the surviving parts of a Tudor country house, and Hidcote, where Lawrence Johnston planted hedges and alleys of trees that divide his garden into "rooms," each with its own character.

In England, gardening is a democratic activity. The typical English house, whether a modest country cottage or a semidetached suburban "villa," is as likely as a stately home to have its garden, and concentrated floral color even spills from windowboxes down the featureless faces of vast London apartment blocks. Everywhere, today as in the long millenia of their history, English men and women continue to shape the landscape of their pliable island home. In ways great and small, they go on adding to the country's dense cultural fabric visible evidence of their individual tastes and of their generation's place in history.

Above: Statues of civic and intellectual leaders were erected outside the town hall in Manchester, the leading cultural and commercial city of the English northwest. *Left:* The city's commercial heart was founded on wealth derived from cotton goods.

The wealth of the port city of Liverpool, at the mouth of the Mersey River, has come traditionally from the sea. Heraldic, legendary liver birds appear on the cupolas of dockside buildings. *Below:* St. George's Hall, a grand nineteenth-century space for meetings and concerts, has been called "England's finest public building."

Above: Rievaulx Abbey, Yorkshire, founded by Cistercian monks in 1131, was despoiled by Protestant reformers in the sixteenth century. *Opposite:* Whitby Abbey on the Yorkshire coast is another romantic ruin that was once a monastery.

Above, left to right: Thirsk, a market town in the North Riding of Yorkshire, has been made famous by the veterinarian James Herriot, author of *All Creatures Great and Small.* Sheep dot farm fields in the Vale of York. *Below:* The spires of York Minster can be viewed from the city's still-standing medieval walls. *Opposite:* The Decorated Gothic west front and superb early glass make York Minster the most splendid cathedral in the north of England.

Castle Howard, an eighteenth-century great house in northern Yorkshire, was built in the Italian manner. *Below:* The literary Brontë sisters lived in their father's parsonage in the small, moorside town of Haworth in the mid-nineteenth century.

Kirkstone Pass winds through the Lake District, where England's most rugged mountains rise above fertile river valleys and shimmering basins. *Below:* Castlerigg stone circle, Cumbria, is probably one of the earliest in Britain. *Overleaf:* Structures in Cumbria are made from stone, the most readily available building material on the mountainous farms of the Pennine region.

Above: Chariots once traversed the Northumberland countryside on this arrow-straight Roman road. *Opposite:* Hadrian's Wall, built during the reign of the emperor of that name to keep unruly Celts out of Roman Britain, crosses Northumberland just south of the present Scottish border.

Index of Photography

All photographs courtesy of The Image Bank, except where indicated *.